Mystery Monsters or Real Animals?

Milly Vranes

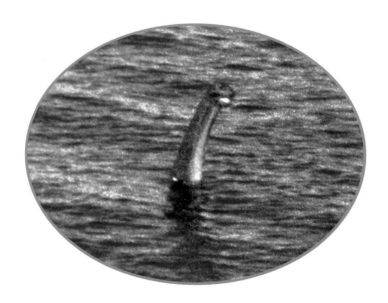

Published by Troll Communications L.L.C.
Reprinted by arrangement with Barrie Publishing Pty Limited,
Suite 513, 89 High Street, Kew, Australia, 3101

ISBN 0 8167 4992 2

Printed in Singapore by PH Productions Pte Ltd
10 9 8 7 6 5 4 3 2 1

Every effort has been made to contact the owners of the
photographs in this book. Where this has not been possible, we
invite the owners of the copyright to notify the publishers.

ANT Photo Library/Bill Bachman p. 19; ANT Photo Library/Grant
Dixon pp. 7, 12; ANT Photo Library/D. Parer p. 5; ANT Photo
Library/Otto Rogge p. 14; ANT Photo Library/Norbert Wu
pp. 20-21; illustration by Biggibilla from Jean Ellis, Dreamtime,
HarperCollins, 1991 p. 18; Fortean Picture Library pp. 4, 5, 8, 9,
13; Fortean Picture Library/Rene Dahinden pp. 16, 17; Fortean
Picture Library/Austin Hepburn p. 10; Fortean Picture
Library/Christopher L. Murphy cover, p. 15; Fortean Picture
Library/A.N. Shiels pp. 1, 22; Fortean Picture Library/Nicholas
Witchell pp. 6, 11.

Contents

Have you ever seen something you can't explain? Something that seems unreal? Some people claim they have seen creatures that cannot be identified. In almost every part of the world, such reports have been made. In Scotland, there is the Loch Ness monster; in Tibet and Nepal, the Abominable Snowman; in America, Bigfoot; and in Australia, the Bunyip.

The only evidence of these creatures is poor-quality photographs and faded footprints. There is no positive proof that these creatures exist. However, this does not mean that they don't exist.

Many years ago, sailors believed in mermaids. They believed mermaids were women who lived in the ocean. We now think that these sailors saw dugongs, also called sea cows. Dugongs are large, aquatic mammals that feed on plants. They have small flippers and no hind legs. In the water, they can look like heavy, half-fish people!

What about other mysterious creatures? Are they animals yet to be discovered, animals thought to be extinct, or mysterious monsters? It is possible that they are just waiting to become a part of the known animal kingdom.

The Loch Ness Monster

Loch Ness is one of the largest lakes in Scotland. The first record of a monster in the lake was written down in 565. In Saint Columba's biography, he tells of a swimmer who was killed by a hungry lake monster. Although there were many ancient legends about monsters, this account made the Loch Ness monster famous.

When a new road was built along the edge of the lake in 1933, the number of sightings of the monster soared. In 1934, a young veterinary student was riding a motorcycle. He claimed that he nearly ran into the monster as it crossed the road.

Most sightings made by people seem to agree that the monster looks like a plesiosaur. Plesiosaurs were aquatic reptiles that lived from the Triassic period to the Jurassic period. This was about 230–144 million years ago. The plesiosaur had a roundish, bulky body and tapering tail. It had a long neck and a small head. It also had two flippers that helped to propel it through the water.

Probably one of the first photographs of the monster was taken in 1933 by a man named Hugh Gray. He said that he did not see any head, but that there was a lot of movement in the water.

The "surgeon's photograph" is probably the most famous picture of the monster. In 1993, though, a man named Christian Spurling admitted that the photograph was a fake. He had helped build the model monster that was photographed.

On a clear day in August 1996, Austin Hepburn saw movement in the waters of Loch Ness. The photographs he took show a wake. There was no wind that day. No boats were in the area.

Many scientists have tried to find out whether the monster really exists. Sonar and other high-tech equipment have been used. Research is still being carried out to this day. But the water of the lake is dark and murky. This makes it difficult to take any clear pictures. No conclusive evidence has ever been found to prove or disprove the legend.

However, one investigation helped to fuel the mystery. Something very large was detected under the water, but scientists still cannot agree on what their equipment detected.

Can it be possible that a prehistoric creature still exists beneath the deep and murky waters of Loch Ness?

The Yeti

Even in remote, snow-covered areas, there are reports of mysterious creatures. The Abominable Snowman, also known as the Yeti, is said to be a hairy, apelike creature. It is supposed to be much taller than a man. It is said to live in the Himalayas, mostly near Tibet and Nepal. The Himalayas, in southern Asia, is the highest mountain range in the world.

Even though there have been expeditions to find this creature, no evidence has been found. This could be because it is difficult to track anything in this steep and frozen region. Or it could be because no such creature exists.

Like the Loch Ness monster, the Yeti is linked to a creature of the past— *Gigantopithecus.* This was a large primate that lived in the Pleistocene age, about two million years ago. It is this creature that some people believe still lives in the mountain ranges.

The only signs of the Yeti ever found have been footprints. Scientists say that the footprints were probably made by bears.

Sometimes when bears walk, they place their hindfeet into the imprints of their forefeet. This makes a very big, apelike footprint.

Also, all the tracks found were in snow. If a bear leaves footprints in the snow and some of the snow melts, the tracks appear to be bigger than they are. People can then mistake these footprints for the footprints of the Yeti.

The only way scientists will accept the footprints as those of the Yeti is if the tracks found are fresh. Maybe in time, fresh tracks of the Yeti will be found.

Sasquatch

Is this Bigfoot?

Reports of other huge, apelike creatures come from northwestern North America. In forests from California to British Columbia, sightings of a big, hairy creature have been reported.

In North America, this creature is called Bigfoot because its footprints are said to be so large. The Native Americans of Canada call it Sasquatch. Sasquatch means wild men.

Sasquatch is usually described as having reddish-brown fur, being muscular, and walking upright. Explorers and lumberjacks are among those who say they have seen the creature. Again, no real evidence, such as fur, has been found.

The only traces of Sasquatch have been footprints. A British explorer is sometimes credited with finding the first footprints of a Sasquatch in 1811. The footprints differ in shape from the print of a human. They also differ from those of bears and apes.

The footprints are not accepted as evidence. Some people say that they were made by practical jokers. Two people have admitted that they once made footprints in the woods. But some footprints have been found in remote mountain areas where only trained mountaineers can go.

Casts taken of footprints — could they belong to Bigfoot?

In 1967, a man named Roger Patterson took some film footage of what was believed to be a Sasquatch. He said that he saw a female Sasquatch and filmed her running through the woods. The film is not clear enough to be believable. Many people think that it is a hoax. They believe that what the film shows is someone dressed up in an ape suit.

The Bunyip

The bunyip is reported to be a big, furry creature. It is said to look something like a hippopotamus and live in lagoons in Australia.

Many people believe that it is just a creature of myth. However, respected explorers have reported sighting this unexplained creature. Others report that the creature looked like a hippopotamus with a long neck. The creature has been said to make booming or roaring noises. A fantastic version is shown in the art of Aboriginal people.

Some people believe that the bunyip can be explained by the possible presence of seals.

Myth or reality? It is hard to say.

19

The Coelacanth

It is possible that some prehistoric creatures exist without people knowing. An example of this is the giant fish called the coelacanth. Scientists had studied the fossil remains of this fish. It was believed to be extinct since prehistoric times. Yet, in 1938, a live coelacanth was pulled from a fishing net.

Further research showed that this fish was living in the deep waters off the African coast. This finding helped scientists to compare this fish with modern-day fish. It helped them to make theories about how fish, and perhaps humans, evolved.

If a fish thought extinct for many millions of years was found alive, then it is possible that there are other animals living that we do not know about.

What Do You Think?

Mystery monsters or real animals? No one knows. There is only one thing that all these creatures have in common, and that is that someone, somewhere, believes in them.

Investigations continue, but whether they will lead to new discoveries is yet to be seen. Until real evidence is found, these mysterious creatures will remain just that: mystery monsters.

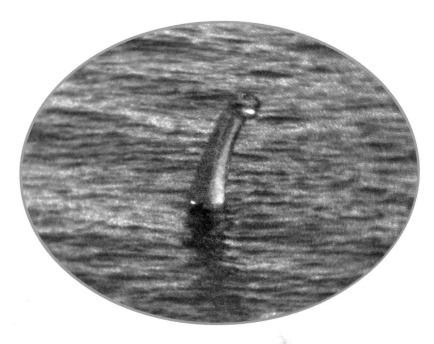

Glossary

ancient	of great age
conclusive	having the ability to prove, without question
evidence	unquestionable proof
extinct	having no living representatives
hoax	an attempt to trick someone
mysterious	puzzling or hard to explain; full of mystery
prehistoric	before recorded history
primate	a mammal of the group that includes humans, apes, monkeys, etc.
remote	distant and isolated
sonar	a method of using echoes to locate objects in water
tapering	gradually thinner at one end
veterinary	of the medical treatment of animals

Index